KT-217-022

SCIENCE MISSIONS

Cloning Pets

Sean Stewart Price

Raintree is an imprint of Capstone Global Library Limited, a company incorporated in England and Wales having its registered office at 7 Pilgrim Street, London, EC4V 6LB – Registered company number: 6695582

First published in hardback in 2011

Edited by Adam Miller, Andrew Farrow, and Adrian Vigliano
Designed by Philippa Jenkins
Original illustrations © Capstone Global Library Ltd (2011)
Illustrated by KJA-artists.com
Picture research by Tracy Cummins
Production control by Alison Parsons
Originated by Dot Gradations
Printed and bound in China by South China Printing Company Ltd

ISBN 978 1 406217 54 4 (hardback)
14 13 12 11 10
10 9 8 7 6 5 4 3 2 1

British Library Cataloguing in Publication Data
Price, Sean Stewart
Cloning pets. – (Science missions)
636'.0821-dc22
A full catalogue record for this book is available from the British Library.

Acknowledgements
We would like to thank the following for permission to reproduce photographs: AP Photo/John Chadwick p.**9**; Corbis ©EPA/GARY I ROTHSTEIN pp.**4–5**; Corbis ©Lester V. Bergman p.**7 top**; Corbis ©Najlah Feanny p.**8**; Corbis ©Jim Richardson p.**17**; Corbis ©GARY I ROTHSTEIN/epa p.**20**; Corbis ©zhou qi/XinHua/Xinhua Press p.**23**; Corbis ©Reuters p.**26**; Corbis ©JO YONG-HAK/Reuters p.**34**; Corbis ©Stewart Cohen p.**38**; Corbis ©Sanford/Agliolo p.**39**; Corbis ©RBM Online/Handout/Reuters p.**43**; Corbis ©Steve & Ann Toon/Robert Harding World Imagery p.**47**; FLPA ©Hugh Clark p.**45**; Getty Images/GABRIEL BOUYS/AFP p.**22**; Getty Images/Texas A&M University p.**27**; Getty Images/Peter Sherrard pp.**32–33**; Getty Images/Steve Gorton and Tim Ridley p.**35**; Getty Images/Paul Nicklen p.**36**; Getty Images/Erik Sampers p.**37**; Getty Images/Chip Somodevilla p.**48**; istockphoto ©Dan Brandenburg p.**21**; istockphoto ©paul kline pp.**18–19**; Mary Evans/ITC/LEW GRADE/PRODUCERS CIRCLE/Ronald Grant Archive p.**42**; Photo Researchers, Inc./Russell Kightley pp.**10–11**; Photo Researchers, Inc./BSIP p.**13**; Photo Researchers, Inc./Professor Miodrag Stojkovic p.**15**; Photo Researchers, Inc./Gusto p.**28**; Photo Researchers, Inc./Hybrid Medical p.**29**; Photo Researchers, Inc./Philippe Psaila p.**30**; Photo Researchers p.**44**; Photo Researchers, Inc./Mark Newman p.**46**; Shutterstock ©Gilles DeCruyenaere p.**7** bottom; Shutterstock ©Andresr p.**12**; Shutterstock ©HomeStudio pp.**50–51**; THE KOBAL COLLECTION/LUCASFILM/20TH CENTURY FOX pp.**24–25**; THE KOBAL COLLECTION/MBLIN/UNIVERSAL pp.**40–41**.

Cover photograph of two cloned beagles reproduced with permission of Getty Images.

We would like to thank Ann Fullick for her invaluable help in the preparation of this book.

CONTENTS

Some words are printed in bold, **like this**. You can find out what they mean by looking in the glossary. You can also look out for them in the **WORD STORE** box at the bottom of each page.

SEND IN THE CLONES

In January 2009 Sir Lancelot Encore became one of the world's most expensive dogs. He cost his owners £103,700.

Why? Because Encore is a **clone** – an exact copy of another living thing. A clone is a copy because it shares the same **genes** as another plant or animal. Genes are the instructions for life found within our cells. Genes decide if something grows into a gerbil or a geranium or a girl.

Encore's owners had lost their original Labrador retriever, Sir Lancelot, to illness in January 2008. So, they asked a company called BioArts to take some of the dog's cells. The company used those cells to make Encore, the clone. But cloning is very complicated and time-consuming. That is why it is so expensive.

Encore is one of the first cloned dogs in the United States. The question is: Will there be more like him? The price of pet cloning is falling. But it is still not clear if people will want to clone their pets. If they do, what will that mean for other pets? What will it mean for other animals? What will it mean for people?

Sir Lancelot Encore at 10 weeks old.

How common is cloning?

To many people, cloning still sounds like an idea out of science fiction. Yet humans have been experimenting with cloning for at least 4,000 years.

Making an exact **genetic** copy of a plant is pretty easy. Farmers can take a twig or cutting from one plant and **graft** it onto another. In some cases, if they also root the twig in water, it will grow. In fact, the word *clone* comes from the Greek word meaning "twig". Many common plants are grown this way, including chrysanthemums and Red Delicious apples. There is nothing controversial about it.

This diagram shows the basic process of plant cloning. Cells from the root are placed in an artificial environment called a culture. They develop into masses of cells called calluses, which can eventually develop as new plants.

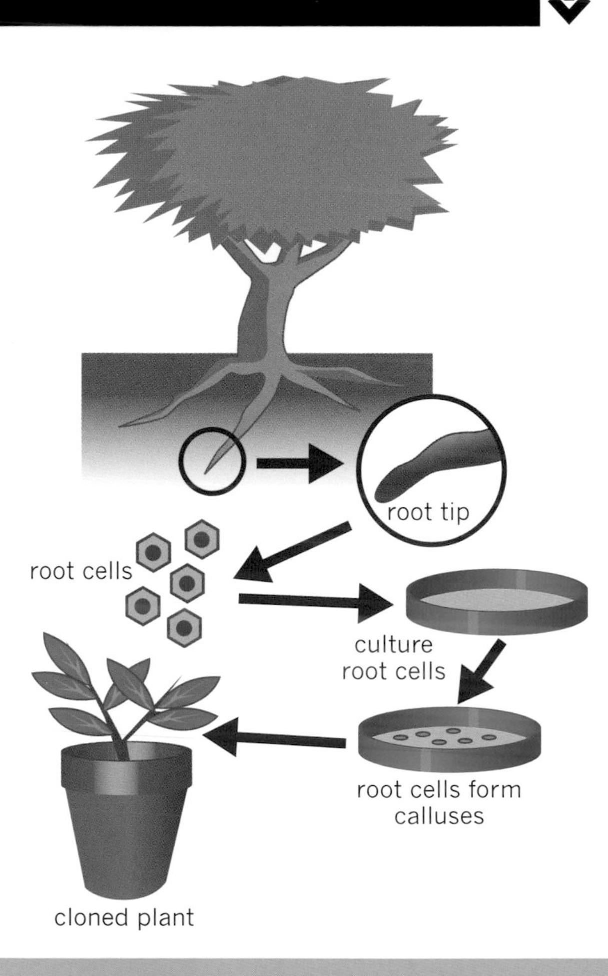

In nature, simple animals can also clone themselves. Some science books show planarian worms. You can cut these worms into three pieces. Each piece will grow into a separate worm. But each worm will be a clone of the original. (Don't try this on other worms – it is cruel and it will not work.)

How to clone a frog

Cloning plants or simple animals can be done by just about anyone. But cloning complicated animals requires scientific know-how. From the 1950s to the 1970s, a series of experiments led to cloned frogs. Frog eggs were chosen to clone because, although very tiny, they are big compared to **mammal** eggs.

WORD STORE

embryo animal in the early stages of development
graft attach

How was the cloning done? Scientists used a thin glass tube called a pipette to suck the **nucleus** from the frog egg. The nucleus is the part of the cell that contains an animal's genetic information. Then they took the nucleus from another cell and transplanted it into the egg cell. Then the egg cell was put inside a frog to see if a baby could be grown.

Embryos, not adults

Like all animal cloning, the process was difficult and led to many failures. These failures led scientists to an important conclusion. They believed that **embryo** cells could be cloned, but that the cells of adult animals could not be cloned. This idea held firm until the mid-1990s. That is when it was disproved by a sheep called Dolly.

Planarian worms can be cloned simply by splitting.

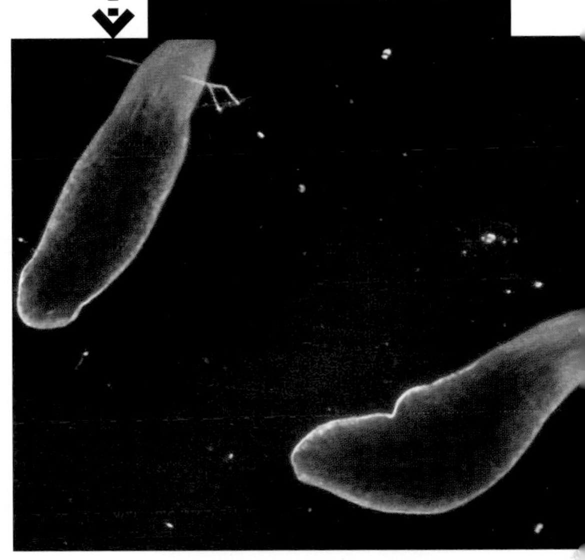

Cloning more complicated animals, like this leopard frog, is a much trickier job.

WORD STORE

mammal animal that makes milk for its young
nucleus control centre of a cell, it also contains DNA

Dolly the cloned sheep.

Dolly's world

5 July 1996 proved to be a landmark day for cloning. In a shed near Roslin, Scotland, a group of scientists gathered to watch a lamb being born. The lamb weighed just over 6.35 kilograms (14 pounds) and had the usual grey-white wool. But this was no ordinary animal. In fact, Dolly – as the lamb was called – was about to become the world's most famous sheep.

Dolly was a clone. To clone Dolly, Scottish scientists Ian Wilmut and Keith Campbell used a cell taken from an adult Finn Dorset sheep. (See page 16 for more on the process of cloning from adult animal cells.) But creating Dolly highlighted the great difficulty in making any clone. The process of cloning a cell is delicate and can only take place under ideal conditions. Dolly's birth came after 276 failed attempts.

WORD STORE

primate group of animals that includes monkeys, apes, and humans

Dolly lived for six years, which is about half the life span of a normal sheep. She died of a lung disease that usually strikes much older sheep. Dolly was also badly overweight and suffered from arthritis. These health issues might have been caused by the fact that she was cloned or they might have been caused by other factors. Nobody is sure. However, during her life, Dolly gave birth to several of her own healthy lambs. That proved that clones could reproduce normally.

Scientists Keith Campbell (middle) and Ian Wilmut (right) stand with Dolly, the clone they created. Also pictured is Dr Ron James (left), the director of an organization that helped the scientists in their work.

Join the club

Since Dolly's birth, scientists have cloned many more animals. They include mice, rats, rabbits, goats, pigs, cattle, mules, horses, cats, and dogs. But, as with Dolly, each success took place after many failures. It often takes hundreds of tries before scientists can produce one successful clone. Some animals remain a puzzle. For instance, scientists still have not been able to clone a **primate** like a monkey or ape.

Cloned plants and animals have been around in nature for thousands of centuries. But Dolly changed the way we look at cloning. Suddenly, scientists could clone a large mammal in a way that could not happen in nature. Cloning large living things like birds, cows, and even humans was no longer the stuff of science fiction.

HOW TO MAKE A CLONE

Cells are life's building blocks. People, sheep, and dogs are all made up of trillions of cells. Each cell is alive. Each cell within you grows, gathers fuel, reproduces, and dies.

Each cell contains a blueprint, or set of instructions. That blueprint determines whether you will be a person, a sheep, or a dog. It also helps determine how you will grow, for example, the colour your skin will be or the length of your arm bones. (But keep in mind that these are also partly determined by environmental factors, like diet and sun exposure.)

A cell's **nucleus** is its control centre. The nucleus of just one cell within you contains all the information needed to recreate a copy of you. That is the information used to make a **clone**.

In some ways, the cloning process is very easy to understand. But cloning is extremely hard to pull off in practice. Scientists fail at it far more often than they succeed.

This diagram shows a cross-section of a cell. This helps to show how complex a single cell is!

Natural-born clones

Can animals produce clones naturally? Yes. We even have a name for them: twins.

There are two kinds of twins. Fraternal twins are created when two different eggs are **fertilized** around the same time. These types of twins are not clones.

Identical twins are created when an **embryo** splits at an early stage of development. This creates two of exactly the same embryo. Identical twins are **genetically** identical. They are natural clones.

Natural twins are common in the animal kingdom. They can be found among cats, sheep, ferrets, deer, cattle, armadillos, and others. So, creating clones of animals is not something unusual in nature.

But the clones made in laboratories are called **artificial** clones. Clones are in many ways just like twins. But instead of being born at the same time, they can be born many years apart.

Natural twins are born to humans as well as animals. These twins are identical.

WORD STORE

artificial something that is human-made
fertilize when an egg combines with male reproductive material

SOMETHING ABOUT TWINS

Many people believe that human twins share a special connection with each other. Studies have shown that twins often share many of the same likes and dislikes. This is true even of twins who are separated at birth. Would that be the same for clones?

Twins expert Nancy Segal said that much of twins' shared behaviour is tied to their common **genes**. But it is also tied to their environment. Identical twins are raised during the same period of time. They are exposed to similar music, TV programmes, news events, and so on.

Segal said that clones would probably not behave in the same way as identical twins. "Born 20 years apart, or even 10 years apart or 5 years apart, it is much more likely that clones would be different," she said. "Because they would be coming to the world at different points in time."

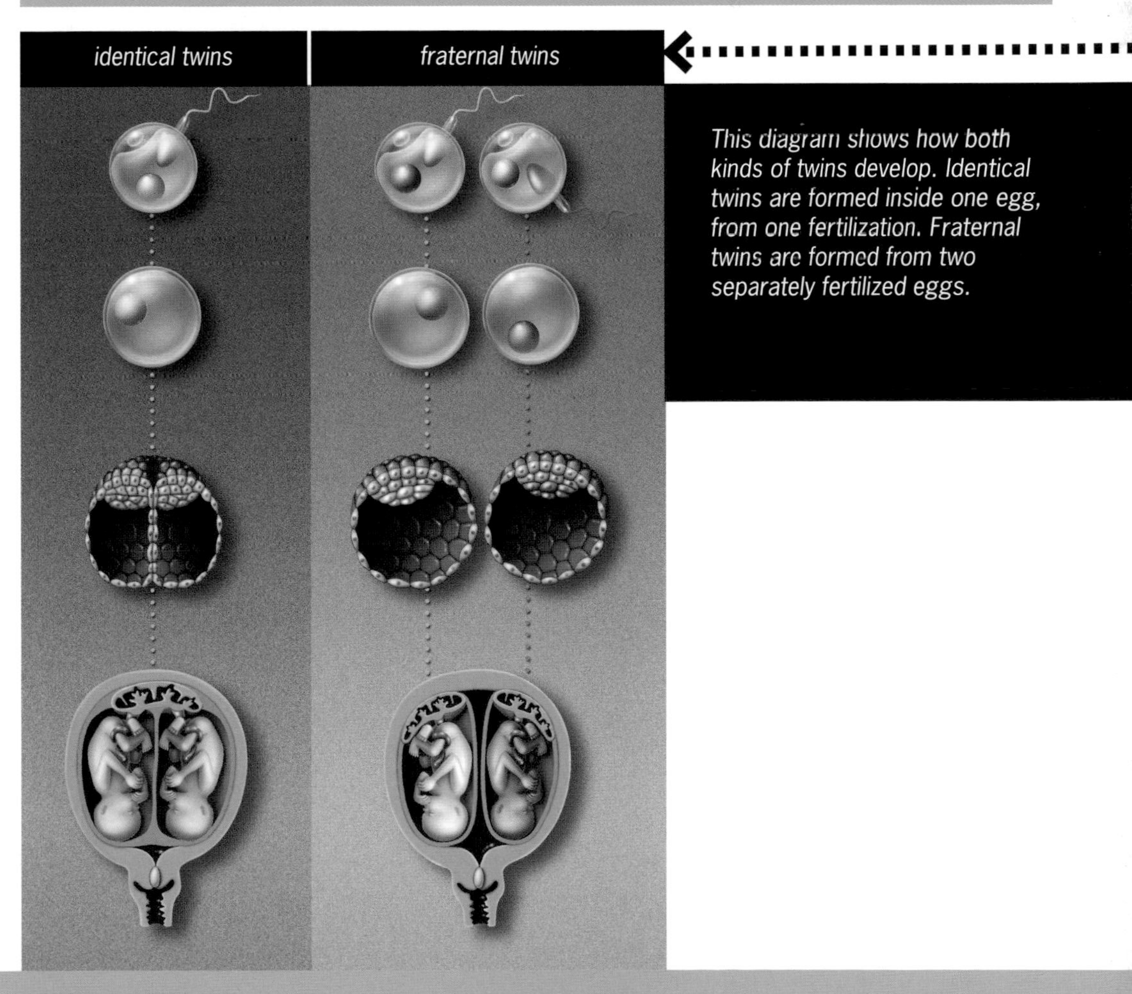

This diagram shows how both kinds of twins develop. Identical twins are formed inside one egg, from one fertilization. Fraternal twins are formed from two separately fertilized eggs.

WORD STORE

gene an instruction for life, found within cells
genetic relating to genes

Artificial cloning

People hear the word *cloning* and think that it applies to one process. But artificial cloning is actually three completely different processes.

Reproductive cloning

The best-known type of artificial cloning is **reproductive cloning**, which is the type of cloning that gave us Encore and Dolly. This technology creates an animal that has the same **DNA** as another animal.

WHAT IS DNA?

WHAT IS DNA?

DNA is short for "deoxyribonucleic acid". The DNA within a cell's nucleus carries the instructions for how a body is made up. Each gene is a section of DNA carrying specific instructions, such as giving a dog spotted or white fur.

WHAT IS THE CELL'S NUCLEUS?

Genes are the most basic unit of heredity. The nucleus of a human cell has around 25,000 of them arranged on 23 pairs of chromosomes. Half of the genes carry the traits (characteristics) you inherit from your mum, the other half from your dad. The genes work together in pairs to produce these traits. A few genes can produce a single trait, such as dimples or ear lobes that dangle. But most genes affect several different things about the way your body works.

Therapeutic cloning

The cloning of human embryos for research is called **therapeutic cloning**. The goal is not to create cloned human beings. Instead, this kind of cloning is used to mass-produce a special kind of cell called a stem cell. Stem cells are taken from an egg after it has divided for five days.

Stem cells are important because they can be used to create any type of cell in the human body. Researchers hope that stem cells could be used to create replacement cells to treat heart disease, cancer, and other conditions. However, this process destroys the embryo. Some people object to stem cell research for that reason.

WORD STORE

heredity refers to passing on traits from one generation to another

An electron microscope captured this image of human stem cells.

Gene cloning

One way of reproducing individual genes is through **gene cloning**. These genes can then be added to the genetic material of bacteria or other organisms in a process called **genetic engineering** or genetic modification.

This type of technology has been around since the 1970s. It can be used to study genes that pass on **inherited** diseases, such as cystic fibrosis. This type of cloning is not particularly controversial.

WORD STORE **inherit** to receive a trait from genes

How to clone a cat

So, how would scientists clone an animal? They must follow a multi-step process. Like all scientific processes, this one has a technical name. Scientists call it somatic cell nuclear transfer. Somatic cells are cells that have nothing to do with reproduction, for example, skin cells or bone cells. So, somatic cell nuclear transfer means moving the nucleus of a somatic cell to an egg. These steps show the process of cloning a cat:

1. First, you need two cats. The first cat will have its cells cloned. The other, an adult female, will provide an unfertilized egg.
2. Take the skin cells of the cat to be cloned. At the same time, take an unfertilized egg cell from the female. Remove the nucleus from that egg.
3. Place the skin cell of the first cat (the cat to be cloned) next to the nucleus-free egg. Zap them with electricity. If everything goes well – and it often does not – this will cause the skin cell to fuse (join) with the empty egg to form a new cell.
4. If it works, this process will create an early-stage embryo. The embryo is **implanted** in a third cat, a female. The cat that carries this embryo is called the **surrogate** mother (see box).
5. The clone is born to the surrogate mother.

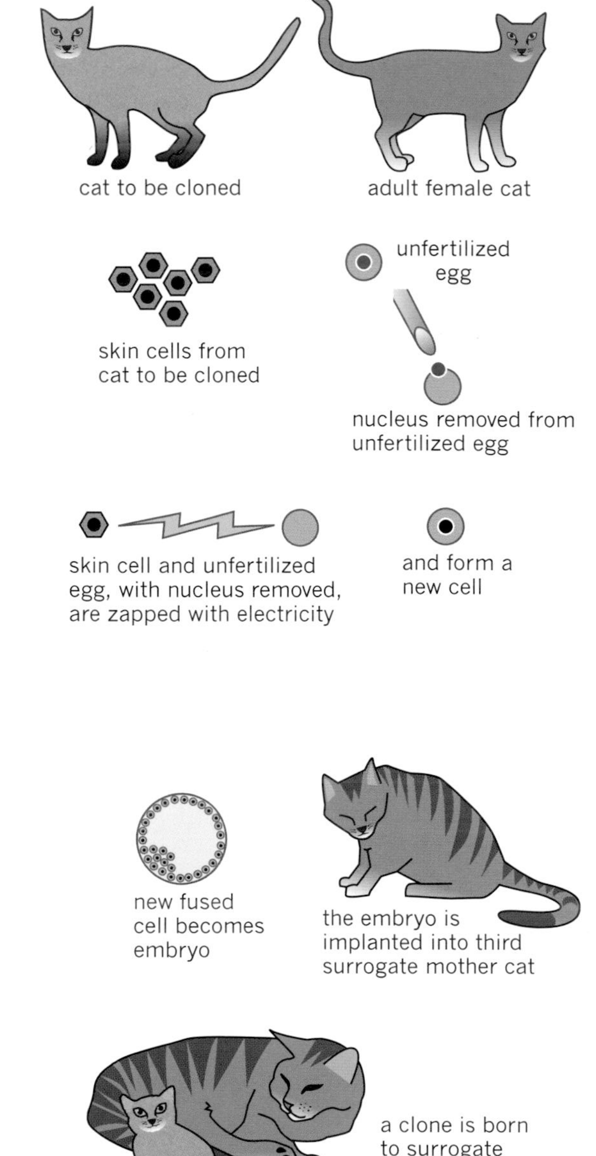

WORD STORE

implant to insert, usually using surgery
surrogate a substitute

SURROGATE MOTHERS

Surrogate means "substitute". The clone's mother is a surrogate because she carries the baby and gives birth to it. However, unlike most babies, the clone baby carries none of her genes. The surrogate mother merely gives birth to the clone.

Cloning Dolly paved the way for many advances in cloning technology. These are cloned cows on a farm in Wisconsin, USA.

WHY CLONE?

Why would someone **clone** an animal? Why go to all the trouble? Why go to all the expense?

There are two main reasons. They are the reasons that people own animals in the first place – love and money.

Humans love their pets. In 2008 the Pet Food Manufacturers Association found there were 7.3 million dogs and 7.2 million cats in the United Kingdom. That same year, there were an estimated 82 million cats and 72 million dogs in the United States, according to the American Veterinary Medical Association. Both countries are also home to millions of fish, gerbils, hamsters, mice, and other small creatures. Other people have more exotic pets.

Some people make their money by selling pets and farm animals. These people often produce and train special breeds. Dogs that are expert trackers fetch a high price. The same is true of cows that produce a lot of meat. Cloning might be expensive at the moment. But as it becomes less expensive, cloning animals might bring people a big profit.

For the love of an animal

Sir Lancelot Encore was born into a very pet-friendly family. Edgar and Nina Otto are the Florida couple who had Encore created in 2009. At the time, they already owned 9 other dogs, 10 cats, 6 sheep, and 4 parrots.

The Ottos had loved Sir Lancelot, the original Labrador retriever. When the first Sir Lancelot became ill in 2003, they took a small amount of **genetic** material from him. They had those cells frozen and then looked for a company to clone him. The Ottos were encouraged by news in 2005 that the first cloned dog, Snuppy, had been born in South Korea. They also did not mind when the price tag for cloning Sir Lancelot came in at £103,700.

The Ottos with Sir Lancelot Encore. Nina Otto shows a picture of Sir Lancelot.

WHY DO PEOPLE OBJECT?

Most animal-rights groups oppose cloning. They have two main objections:

1. The cloning process can be dangerous for the animals involved (see page 30).
2. There is a massive pet over-population problem already.

"There can be no justification for cloning animals to improve performance, or for 'recreating' a pet," said a representative from the Royal Society for the Prevention of Cruelty to Animals (RSPCA). "The process involves subjecting animals to painful and distressing procedures, and there are thousands of unwanted cats and dogs who could be given a loving home instead."

Critics argue that people shouldn't be making clones of pets, when there are already enormous numbers of animals that need homes.

Some people said the Ottos wasted their money. Critics said that their money could have helped thousands of already-living pets in animal shelters. The RSPCA in the United Kingdom and the Humane Society of the United States both condemn the practice of pet cloning.

"We recognize that a person may have an extraordinary bond with an animal, and we encourage the development of these bonds," a Humane Society spokesman said about pet cloning. "But, the fact is, there is no way to create a pet identical to the one who is gone. They are distinctive, and cloning cannot eliminate their uniqueness."

But the Ottos did not want just any dog. They wanted a copy of Sir Lancelot. "He was a wonderful dog," said Nina Otto, 66. "Money wasn't an object. We just wanted our wonderful, loving dog back."

Cloning for money

For centuries, humans have bred animals to make them more useful. Selective breeding means controlling how an animal reproduces. Fast horses have been bred with other fast horses to make even faster horses. Pigs and cows have been bred to increase their meat. Some types of dog have been bred for their alertness and sense of smell.

Many people believe that cloning is simply another way for people to breed animals. For example, in June 2009 the world was introduced to five German Shepherd puppies. But these were not just any young dogs. They were clones of Trakr. Trakr became famous after the terrorist attacks of 11 September 2001. He helped to locate the last human survivor in the rubble of New York's World Trade Center. Trakr himself died in April 2009.

"If the clone has Trakr's abilities, then of course we'll put him into service as a detection dog," said Trakr's former master. That would make Trakr's clones very valuable dogs.

Selective cloning

Many supporters believe that this is the strongest argument for animal cloning. Breeders could select those dogs that are the keenest sniffers to be cloned. The same is true of the fastest horses and meatiest pigs. Once cloned, these animals could be bred with others to produce even better working animals. Cloning would just be one more helpful tool for animal breeders.

The five clones of Trakr. The clones were born to different surrogates over a series of months. This is why they aren't all the same age.

WORD STORE

DNA substance within a cell's nucleus that carries instructions for how a body is made up

Many people confuse cloning with **genetic engineering**. But genetic engineering is different. In genetic engineering, scientists change the **genes** within the **DNA** coding of a plant or animal. For instance, mice can be genetically engineered to carry disease-causing genes. Much of what we know about disease has come from studying animals such as mice.

But cloning can also play a role in this research. It is time-consuming and expensive to breed these animals. Cloning these special mice would shorten the time needed to create more of them. Cloning would also give scientists a population of identical mice to study. That would make it easier for them to tell which cures work and which do not.

This type of cloning could work for bigger animals as well. For instance, many cows, sheep, and goats are genetically engineered to produce ingredients for medicines, including some that could fight blood diseases. Cloning these animals would produce larger herds more quickly. That would allow companies to produce more medicines.

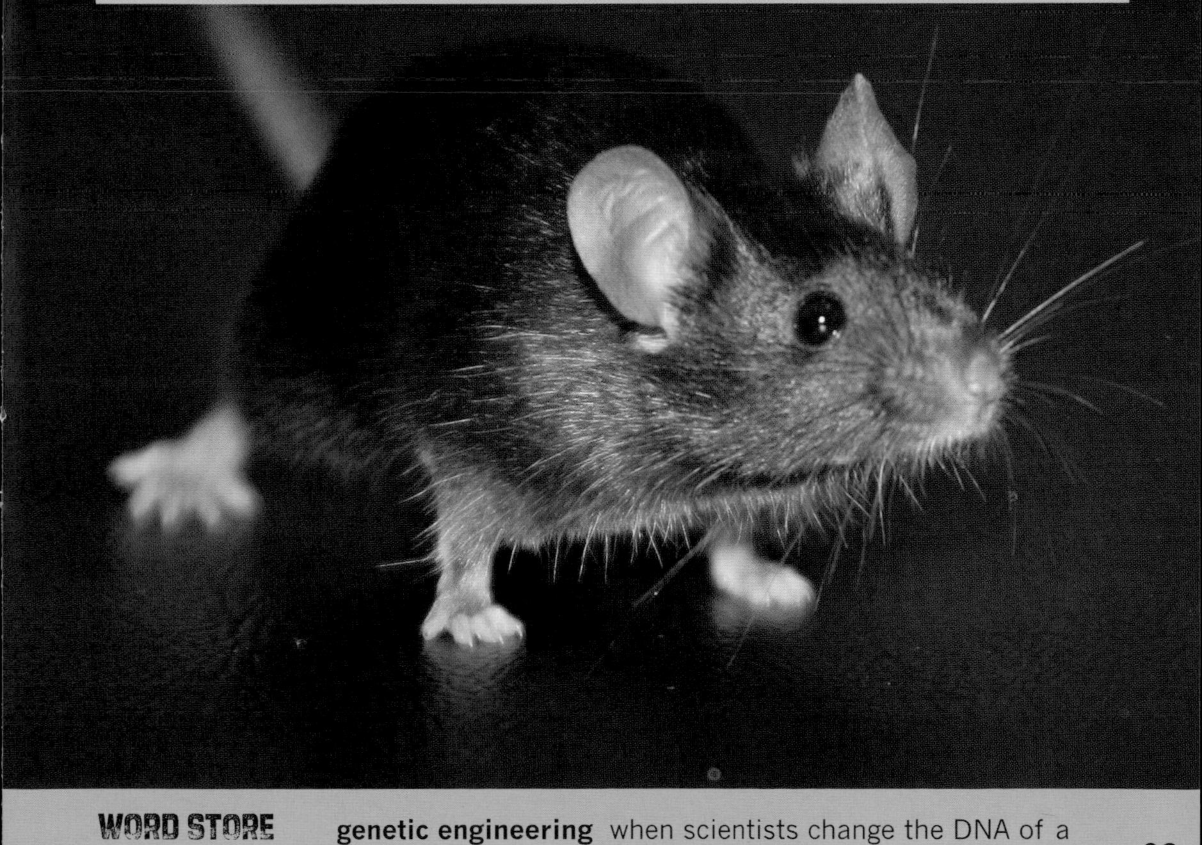

WORD STORE

genetic engineering when scientists change the DNA of a plant or animal

WHAT COULD GO WRONG?

In early 2009, BioArts International seemed ready to cash in on pet **cloning**. BioArts had produced the clone of Sir Lancelot, and it expected a flood of orders for more cloned dogs. "Millions of people think their dog or cat is unique," said Lou Hawthorne, the company's chief executive officer. "A business is based on demand, and there's a huge pent-up demand for this."

Then something strange happened. BioArts offered a "Golden Clone Giveaway". The winner could have his or her dog cloned for free. The media, such as newspapers and television stations, covered this story widely. BioArts expected tens of thousands of people to enter. "We were astonished when just 237 people signed up for the giveaway," Hawthorne said. This clearly meant that there was little demand for dog cloning.

Lack of demand is one big reason that BioArts stopped cloning dogs in 2009. But there are other reasons as well. Some of those reasons have to do with flaws in the technology. Others have to do with the simple fact that cloning remains misunderstood and unpopular among many people.

Some people have argued that science fiction is partially to blame for people's misunderstandings about clones. In many science fiction stories, cloning is portrayed in frightening ways, like this army of identical, robotic clones!

A second chance?

Genetically, a clone is an exact copy of the original dog, cat, or other creature. Many people believe that this means the clone will look and act exactly like the original. But they are in for a surprise. Clones often look and act very differently from what is expected.

The owners of a Brahman bull named Second Chance found that out the hard way. Second Chance was a clone of a bull named Chance. Chance had been a very calm bull with giant horns about 1 metre (3.3 feet) long. At state fairs, thousands of people lined up to have their picture taken with him.

Chance died in 1998, and Texas A&M University offered to clone this rare breed of bull. The result was Second Chance. He looked just like Chance. But Second Chance was much more aggressive. The new bull stabbed his owner twice with his horns, putting him in hospital.

This shows that **genes** are not the only factor that determines behaviour. An animal's experiences and environment also play a big role in how it grows. Along with genes, these factors help shape an animal's temperament and help determine how well it gets along with people.

Second Chance and his owner.

CC and her surrogate mother.

Switching on the right genes

In some cases the cloned animal does not even look like the original. Take the case of CC. In 2001 CC became the world's first cloned cat (the initials CC stand for "Copy Cat"). But CC did not look like Rainbow, the original cat. Rainbow had black, orange, and white fur. But CC had no orange fur.

As it turns out, one cell can often have different genes for fur colour. Some of these genes are switched on and others are switched off. CC had different genes switched on from Rainbow, which meant she looked different. This switching in genes helps explain why natural-born identical twins sometimes look slightly different from each other.

Cloning and health

Most cloned animals are born healthy and stay that way. Most are able to reproduce and live normal animal lives.

But some clones suffer from odd health problems. For instance, as discussed earlier, Dolly the sheep clone died at age six. That is about half the normal life span for a sheep. Second Chance, the Brahman bull, died at the age of eight – less than half the life span of the bull from which he was cloned. The health issues these animals faced might have had nothing to do with cloning. However, animal cloning is so new that scientists are not sure yet.

About 25 per cent of clones are born with health issues that are not present in the original animal. Many cloned animals start life with enlarged organs (such as the heart and liver), which create serious health problems. Others have **defects** in their immune systems. Some develop arthritis and other joint and skeletal issues. Obesity, or being very overweight, seems to be a common problem. Scientists are still baffled by the dog clone that was supposed to be male but was born female.

Dolly the sheep is now stuffed and on display in a museum in Scotland.

OLD CELLS?

Some health problems might be tied to the use of adult cells in cloning. Each cell has a kind of clock made of something called telomeres (pictured below). Telomeres are pieces of **DNA** that get shorter and shorter each time a cell divides. This telomere clock in adult cells is clearly far ahead of the clock in cells from **embryos**.

This does not mean that clones are born at the same age as the original animal. They are born as babies, just like any other animal. But it does mean that some animals cloned from adult cells might have a shorter life span than other animals.

However, there is a process that allows adult cells to be returned to their embryonic state. Also, not all clones have this problem. Experiments done with mice show that six generations of clones aged normally.

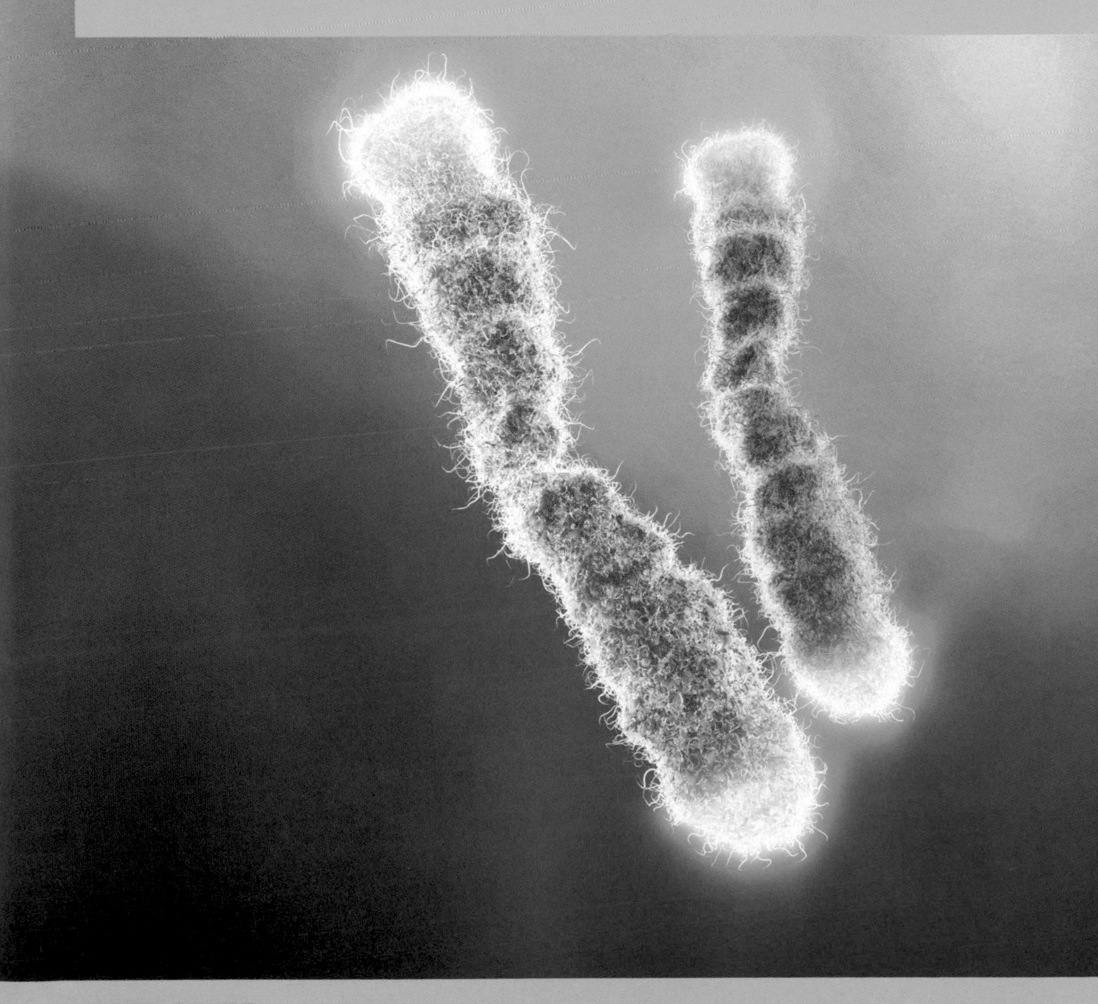

WORD STORE **defect** a problem; something that doesn't work as it should

Cloning is hard on animals

Many people oppose cloning because they believe it hurts animals. For instance, the birth of Dolly only happened after 276 failed attempts. In 2003 scientists tried 716 times to clone rhesus monkeys. Every effort failed. So far, scientists still have not been able to create a **primate** clone. That includes humans.

Many things can go wrong in the cloning process. The cells can fail to divide, or the female carrying the clone can suffer a miscarriage (failed pregnancy). The process can be difficult even with animals that have been successfully cloned. It currently takes at least twelve dogs in order to produce one cloned puppy. The dogs serve either as the donor for the genetic material, the egg donor, or the female who gives birth to the clone. The process of cloning can be stressful for some of these animals. Cloning companies refuse to say how many animals die in the process.

However, people who study cloning say that it is becoming safer all the time. Autumn Fiester is a professor of bioethics, which is the study of moral and legal issues in biology. She said, "Cloning science is advancing so rapidly that the survival rates and general health of clones are beginning to mirror animals naturally conceived." She believes that soon people will have no grounds to make this argument against pet cloning.

A scientist uses a mouth-operated pipette during part of the somatic cell nuclear transfer process.

LITTLE THINGS THAT COUNT

Small things can have a big impact on cell growth. One company found that the way cells are shipped before the cloning process might cause birth defects. Many cells are simply shipped while frozen in ice. Others are shipped in more state-of-the-art containers that keep the temperature steady. The company found that the cells frozen in ice often ended up with abnormal growth. Those shipped the more advanced way were fine.

It has been found that freezing cells in ice may not be the best way to preserve them for cloning.

MYTHS ABOUT CLONES

The very idea of twins can bother some people. Ancient stories from Greece and Rome portray twins or look-alikes as tricksters – people to be feared. In ancient Aztec culture, twins were seen as a direct threat to their parents. Very often, one of the twins would be killed at birth.

Today, twins are less likely to create such anxiety. But the trickster image still lives on. It can be seen in characters like the Weasley twins in the *Harry Potter* series. Twins often seem to be portrayed as getting up to mischief.

This long-held suspicion about twins helps explain in part why **clones** – animal or human – make people uneasy. Clones are basically twins made by science. So, people fear not only the twins. They also fear that nature is being changed in ways that it should not.

Perhaps that is why there are so many myths about cloning. Perhaps that is also why cloning remains unpopular with much of the public.

A clone will have the same memories as the original animal

A clone is a **genetic** copy of an animal. But many people believe that the creation of clones goes beyond just **genes**. They believe that a clone is born with the same thoughts and feelings as the original animal. For example, they believe that if the original animal got its paw stuck in a fence, the clone will have a memory of that experience.

"There are people who contact us thinking that we can basically bring their beloved pet back to life," a cloning company executive said.

Individuals

But clones are individual animals – just as identical twins are individuals. Like any person or animal, a clone's memories are based on experience. A clone grows up with completely different experiences from the original animal. The clone can also grow up in a completely different environment from the original. This means it will have completely different memories. A clone might react to certain events in the same way. For instance, a cloned cat might be an aggressive mouse-catcher like the original. But its memories of mouse catching will be its own.

The dog on the right is a genetically engineered clone. She passed on her genetically engineered traits to her puppy (left), but it is not a clone.

This can get confusing, because genes can have a big impact on an animal's behaviour. For instance, the owners of the bull Second Chance noticed that it behaved a lot like Chance, the original bull. The two animals ate and slept exactly the same way. They did this even though they never met. But Second Chance grew into a very different animal. Chance was gentle enough to be around people. But Second Chance became aggressive easily.

Likewise, people think that the offspring of clones are clones themselves. But cloned animals can reproduce just like any other animals. Their offspring are not clones. They are ordinary baby animals.

CLONING MYTH 2

Clones are unnatural creatures that people should fear

Many people believe that cloning is a new process. They feel that we do not know what to expect from it. In some ways, that is true. In other ways, it is not.

As previously discussed, we have been eating cloned food crops for centuries. A banana takes about 30 years to grow from seed. So, to speed the process along, farmers rely on cloned bananas. The same is true of apples, peaches, grapes, potatoes, and many other crops.

Starfish and many other simple animals already reproduce themselves by cloning. So, cloning can be a very natural process. However, **mammals** and other complex animals have only recently been cloned by scientists.

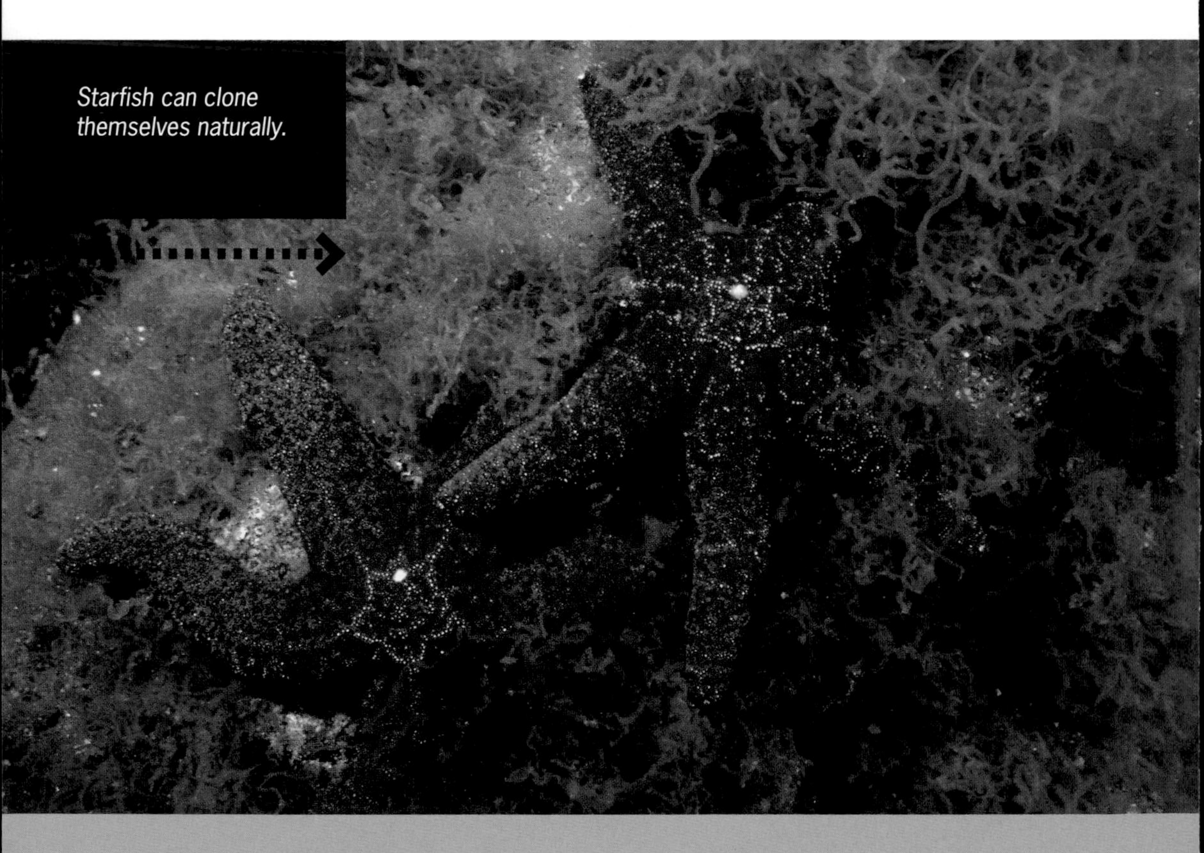

Starfish can clone themselves naturally.

Most animals are born when a male and a female animal come together and make a baby. Cloned animals are created by fusing one cell's **nucleus** with an egg cell that had its nucleus removed.

However, in the cloning process, the egg is **implanted** into a female animal. The clones are then born just like any other animals. They are not grown in a test tube or laboratory.

Many people confuse plant cloning with animal cloning. They believe that a cloned animal's **DNA** has somehow been **grafted** onto another live animal. They fear that cloning is the ability to change one type of live animal into another. This is simply not true.

Bananas are an example of the many food crops that have been cloned by humans.

CLONING MYTH 3

Clones will destroy the diversity of life

Many people who argue that clones will destroy the diversity of life on Earth are worried that clones will not be able to fight diseases.

Many people fear that cloning will harm the **diversity** of life on Earth. People have good reasons to be concerned about diversity. However, cloning is probably not much of a threat.

In nature, animals reproduce when a mother and father come together. This couple produces children. Each child gets a mix of genes from both parents. This creates a population that is diverse (one that has a great variety of different individuals).

Diversity helps all **species** survive in nature. For instance, diversity protects against disease. A disease that hits a diverse population might kill off many individuals. But some individuals will probably have genetic protection against that disease and survive.

If that same disease hit a population of clones, the story might be different. They all have the same genetic information. What if the clones had no protection against the disease? Most or all of the species could be wiped out.

WORD STORE

diversity variety
species group of similar animals that is naturally created

This is a strong argument for maintaining diversity. But scientists say it is not a strong argument against cloning pets. Pet cloning remains expensive. As a result, there are very few cloned animals. The cloned animals that are out there are very different from one another. So, cloning will not hurt diversity among animals.

However, some scientists say that cloning could become a problem in farming. Perhaps if farmers cloned whole flocks of cattle or goats, this might harm diversity. In fact, this is the case with plants – many people currently worry about the lack of diversity among cloned plant crops. However, this is probably unlikely to happen with animals soon. The technology is still too new and the price is still too high.

Some people worry that the cloning of farm animals will eventually lead to larger diversity problems.

EXTREME CLONING

Novels and films often shape public opinion. When it comes to **cloning**, they have had a huge impact. Almost always, their visions of the future show cloning to be a danger – something to be feared.

One of the best-known novels to deal with cloning is Aldous Huxley's *Brave New World* (1932). In it, Huxley presented a grim future world in which humans are mass-produced by cloning. Likewise, the film *Jurassic Park* (1993) turned animal cloning into a nightmare. In the film, a scientist manages to bring back extinct dinosaurs. Then he reproduces them by cloning. At first, this seems like a great idea. But the dinosaurs get out of control and terrorise people.

Many other books and films play on people's fears about cloning. For instance, the *Star Wars* films show clones to be mindless soldiers for the evil emperor. Some of the problems these books and films warn about are unlikely to ever happen. But they are the starting point for many people when talking about cloning issues.

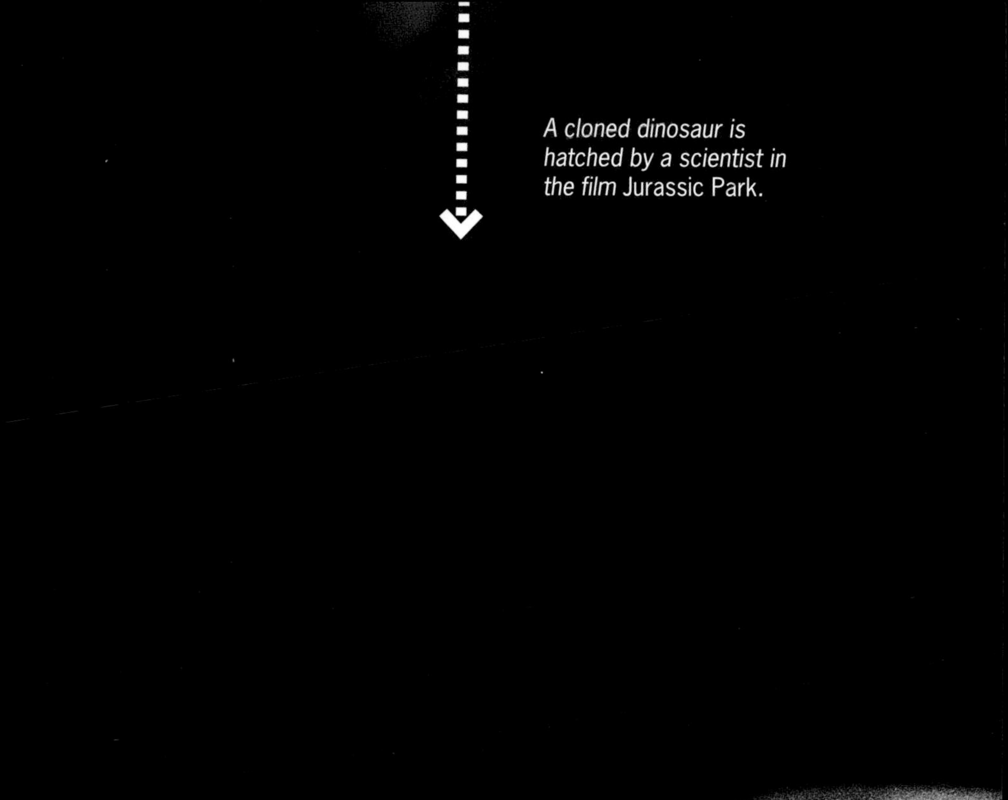

A cloned dinosaur is hatched by a scientist in the film Jurassic Park.

Cloning humans

First in the 1970s and then in the 2000s, scientists claimed to have cloned humans. In both cases, the claims caused a sensation. People feared that human clones would soon become a reality. They feared that the visions out of *Brave New World* or *Star Wars* might soon be possible. But in both cases, the claims proved false.

Some people argue that fears about human cloning are overblown. They point out that human cloning could have a positive impact. For instance, it could allow some couples to finally have children. Some people carry **genetic** illnesses. Cloning could allow a couple in that situation to have children without passing on those illnesses.

Gregory Pence, a professor of philosophy at the University of Alabama in the United States, sees nothing wrong with cloning humans. "If no one is harmed by [cloning], then it raises no moral issue," he said.

This thriller from 1978 was about an evil plot to create dozens of clones of Adolf Hitler!

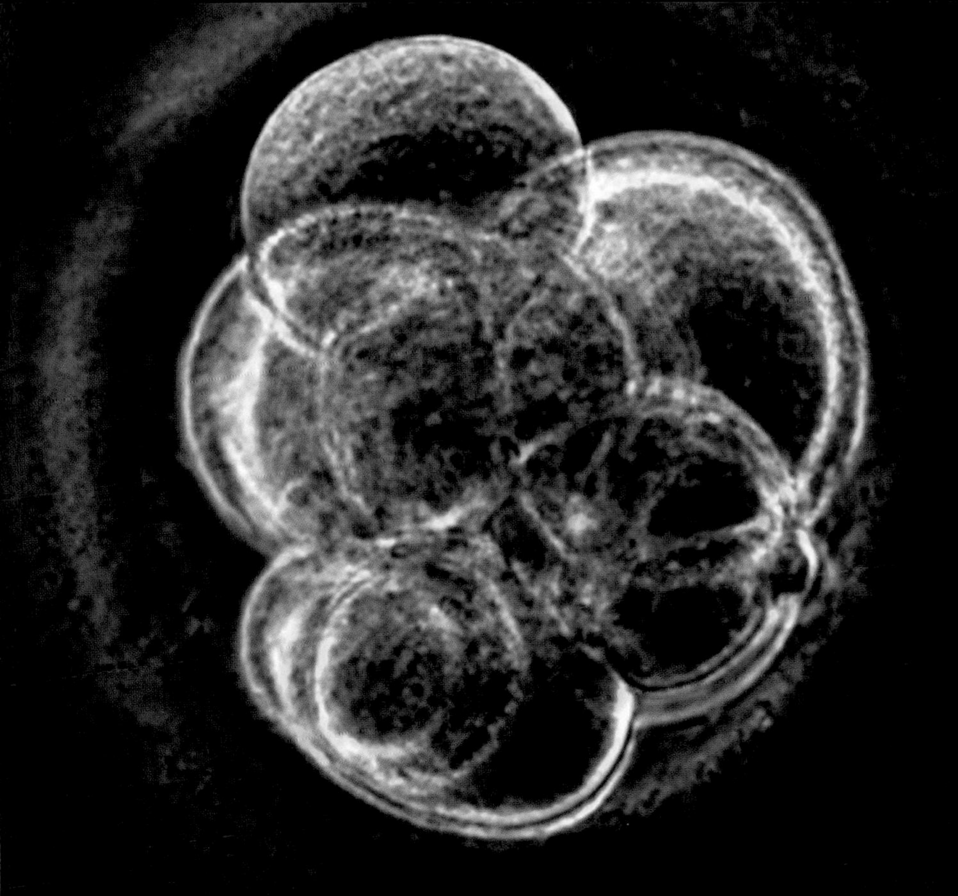

This is a cloned human embryo. Scientists have made major steps towards cloning humans, but a human clone hasn't been born yet.

Opponents of cloning

However, others believe that human **reproductive cloning** is wrong and unnatural. They especially fear that cloning could be merged with **genetic engineering**. This could lead to "designer human beings" who could be mass-produced by cloning. Such technology could erase people's individual identities. Over time, it might even weaken the genetic **diversity** of humans.

These concerns about human cloning are tied to the debate over pet cloning. Many people fear that in time pet cloning will give scientists the know-how to clone humans. They also worry that cloning pets will make people more open to the idea of cloning humans.

"Many people consider pets to be part of our families," said Marcy Darnovsky, associate director of the Center for Genetics and Society. "If we get used to cute cloned puppies, will some people expect cute cloned babies next?"

WORD STORE

reproductive cloning process that creates a new organism by copying the DNA of another organism

Could cloning bring back extinct species?

Three years before Dolly was born, the Steven Spielberg film *Jurassic Park* put cloning in the minds of many people. The film was based on a 1990 best-selling book by Michael Crichton. In the book, a scientist develops an amusement park that features live dinosaurs.

In the story, the dinosaurs are cloned using ancient dinosaur **DNA**. This DNA is obtained in a clever way. The scientist finds a blood-sucking insect that had been fossilized in amber. The amber perfectly preserved the insect from dinosaur times. The scientist uses the dinosaur blood preserved in the insect to recreate the animals and then clone them.

In reality, scientists say this is very unlikely to happen. The insect would have to have been trapped in amber almost immediately after biting a dinosaur. Even then, it is unlikely that the dinosaur blood would have stayed fresh enough to preserve its cells.

Bringing back any extinct **species** by reproductive cloning is possible as an idea. But it would be very difficult to actually do so. Scientists would need a lot of the animal's DNA. That is because cloning has such a high failure rate, as eggs and cells fail to develop properly.

The dodo is a species of bird that became extinct in the late 1600s. If it could be brought back by cloning, do you think it could survive?

This an extinct animal, called a thylacine, or Tasmanian tiger, shown here in a zoo in 1928. This species has been extinct since 1936, after being killed off by humans.

Another reason cloning an extinct animal would be difficult is that an animal must serve as a **surrogate** mother. So far, all surrogates have been similar to the clones. For instance, another sheep gave birth to Dolly. There are some extinct animals with close relatives that are still alive. For example, an elephant might be able to give birth to an extinct woolly mammoth. But could any animal carry and lay a cloned dinosaur egg? Nobody knows.

There are other problems as well. Even if scientists could clone a lot of an extinct species, where would we put them? When an animal dies out, other animals take its place in nature. Would adding a species of clones disrupt this balance? Also, the cloned animals would be born in captivity. How would they learn to survive in the wild?

"Sadly, here is a lesson that every scientist learns, and usually pretty quickly," wrote Rob DeSalle and David Lindley in their book *The Science of Jurassic Park and the Lost World* (1997). "It's easy to have clever ideas, but it's rare to have clever ideas that actually work."

Can cloning help save endangered species?

In 2000 scientists cloned a gaur, a rare type of ox from India. This was the first time an endangered species had been cloned. Since then, scientists have cloned several different endangered species, including breeds of wild sheep and cattle. In 2003 the Audubon Nature Institute in New Orleans, USA, came up with ways to better clone and then breed wild animals. The centre cloned a rare African wildcat that it named Ditteaux (pronounced "ditto", which means "repeat").

But could all this really help endangered species survive? The answer is not clear yet. Some organizations have stored samples of wild animal DNA for many years. The San Diego Zoo has preserved cells from more than 3,200 **mammals** representing 355 species and sub-species (smaller categories of species). Around the world there may be over a million samples representing at least 700 different species. Cloning the cells of some endangered animals might help revive their populations.

These animals are a type of endangered Asian cow called the Javan banteng. In 1980 the San Diego Zoo froze a single skin cell of this species, which was cloned successfully years later. A healthy Javan banteng clone was born to a beef cow surrogate in 2003.

Many species, such as these white rhinos in South Africa, have been pushed close to extinction. Do humans have a responsibility to try everything, even cloning, to help these animals?

Endangered species face many threats. Human activity is destroying wildlife habitats worldwide. Pollution, overhunting, and other threats could wipe out many species. Unless these activities are dealt with, endangered species will remain in serious danger.

Many environmentalists believe that cloning gives people a false sense of hope. They point out that saving endangered species is hard and complicated work. They are afraid that people will see cloning as an easy answer to a much larger problem.

Even so, many scientists agree that cloning can help species "buy time" until conditions improve. "The goal is to use whatever tools we can to help boost these populations," said Betsy Dresser of the Audubon Nature Institute. "While no single approach is going to solve the incredibly complex problem of disappearing wildlife, cloning is critically important in the race against extinction."

PET CLONING AND PUBLIC OPINION

Cost aside, pet cloning remains deeply unpopular with the public. There are few public opinion polls on pet cloning. But all of them show that people overwhelmingly oppose the idea. For instance, a May 2004 Gallup poll of Americans showed that 64 per cent of people disapprove of pet cloning, while only 32 per cent approve.

The Gallup poll showed something else interesting. It found that university-educated people who earn over £50,000 tended to support some types of animal cloning. That appears to be good news for cloning companies. These are the people who would most likely be able to afford pet cloning. But the poll also showed that these people supported animal cloning only for research purposes. Most of them opposed cloning just to recreate a pet.

These people are protesting against the use of cloned cows in the American food system. Many fears remain about the possible dangers of cloning, and people often worry that scientists don't know enough about cloning yet to use cloned animals for food. What do you think?

Will we all own cloned pets one day?

It seems unlikely that one day we will all own cloned pets. This is mostly because of one very big reason: pet cloning is expensive.

Sir Lancelot Encore cost his owners about £103,700. Even though scientists have learned cost-saving measures thanks to the birth of Encore and other animals, cloned pets remain very expensive. The price of cloned dogs has fallen to about £33,500. A cloned cat might cost around £21,000.

But there are other costs to pet cloning. The original pet's cells – the genetic material – must be stored after it dies. This storage is called "**gene** banking". Gene banking a healthy animal's DNA can cost anywhere from £200 to £800. There are usually £67-per-year maintenance fees as well.

The costs of cloning pets will probably fall over time. Scientists will become better and faster at cloning processes. They will find ways to make it cheaper. This is especially true if the demand for cloning pets increases. More and more cloning companies will compete for business. They will have to drop their prices to attract customers.

But cloning remains a highly technical procedure. Only a few skilled scientists can do it. That means pet cloning will probably remain something only rich people can afford for a long time.

Even if the process of cloning pets becomes very cheap, it might not be something everyone wants to do. While some people might choose to clone a pet, other people would probably choose to start a new relationship with a new pet.

PET CLONING TIMELINE

1673 Dutch scientist Anton van Leeuwenhoek becomes the first person to see living cells. He uses a simple microscope that he made himself.

1831 Scottish biologist Robert Brown shows that the nucleus is the most important part of a cell. Some scientists had noticed the nucleus before, but had not thought it was important.

1839 German scientists Theodor Schwann and Mathias Schleiden create the "cell theory of life". It states that all life is made up of cells.

1860s Austrian monk Gregor Mendel studies pea plants to find out how genes control heredity. His work is ignored until the early 1900s. It then becomes the foundation for genetics, the branch of science that deals with heredity.

1952 US scientists Robert Briggs and Thomas J King clone northern leopard frogs using the cells of embryos. These are the first animals to be artificially cloned.

1953 US scientist James Watson and English scientist Francis Crick show the structure of DNA. This discovery paves the way for many other breakthroughs in genetics. It also opens the way for genetic engineering.

1953–1960s Further experiments with frogs improve scientists' knowledge about cloning.

1963 English scientist J B S Haldane coins the word *clone*.

1969 US scientists James Shapiro and Jonathan Beckwith identify the first gene.

1977 Scientists clone mice using the cells of embryos.

1984 Danish scientist Steen Willadsen uses embryo cells to clone sheep. Within two years, other scientists use embryo cells to clone a cow.

1996 Scottish scientists Ian Wilmut and Keith Campbell create Dolly. She is the first clone of a mammal using adult cells instead of the cells of embryos. In the next decade, researchers will clone many farm animals, including cows, pigs, goats, mules, and horses.

1997 The creation of Dolly sparks fears that human reproductive cloning will happen soon. The United Kingdom and 18 other European countries soon ban reproductive cloning on humans. The United States cuts off all public funding for human cloning, and several states ban the practice.

2001 CC, or Copy Cat, becomes the first ever cloned pet. That same year researchers produce a gaur (a type of ox), the first cloned endangered species.

2003 Researchers clone Ditteaux, a rare type of African wildcat.

2004 South Korean scientist Hwang Woo-suk claims that he has cloned a human embryo. His claims later turn out to be false. Despite being disgraced, Hwang and his research team remain key cloners of pets.

2005 Snuppy, the first cloned dog, is born in South Korea.

GLOSSARY

artificial something human-made, as opposed to something from nature

clone biological copy of a plant or animal that shares the same genetic make-up as the original; the word is also used to describe the act of making the genetic copy

defect a problem; something that doesn't work as it should

deoxyribonucleic acid (DNA) substance within a cell's nucleus that carries the instructions for how a body is made up

diversity variety

embryo fertilized egg that has begun dividing into new cells and has had time to mature; an animal in early stages of development

fertilize an egg is fertilized when it comes into contact with male reproductive material. This allows it to begin developing into a new individual.

gene stretch of DNA that carries instructions for life found within cells

gene cloning scientific process in which cloning is used to reproduce copies of genes or segments of DNA. It is widely used to study genes that pass on inherited diseases, such as cystic fibrosis.

genetic relating to genes

genetic engineering process in which scientists change the genes within the DNA coding of a plant or animal

graft attach

heredity the passing on of characteristics from one generation to another

implant to insert, usually by using some kind of surgery

inherit to receive a trait from genes

mammal warm-blooded animal that gives milk to its young and usually has hair or fur

nucleus control centre of a cell, which contains the cell's DNA (or blueprints)

primate group of animals that includes monkeys, apes, and humans

reproductive cloning scientific process that creates an animal with the same DNA as another animal, such as Dolly the sheep

species group of similar animals that is naturally created

surrogate substitute. A clone is implanted into a surrogate, or substitute, mother, who gives birth to it.

therapeutic cloning scientific process in which human embryos are cloned for research, creating stem cells. Researchers hope that stem cells can be used as replacement cells to treat certain diseases.

FIND OUT MORE

BOOKS

From Sea Urchins to Dolly the Sheep: Discovering Cloning, Sally Morgan (Heinemann Library, 2008)

Introduction to Genes and DNA, Anna Claybourne (Usborne, 2006)

The Rough Guide to Genes and Cloning, Jess Buxton and Jon Turney (Rough Guides, 2007)

Science at the Edge: Cloning, Sally Morgan (Heinemann Library, 2009)

WEBSITES

RSPCA's Views on Cloning
www.rspca.org.uk/allaboutanimals/laboratory/biotechnology/clonedanimals
Read the viewpoint of the RSPCA (Royal Society for the Prevention of Cruelty to Animals) on pet cloning.

Dolly's Arthritis
news.bbc.co.uk/1/hi/sci/tech/1742344.stm
This BBC article, written when it was discovered that Dolly the sheep had developed arthritis, looks at some of the issues with animal cloning.

Science News for Kids
www.sciencenewsforkids.org/articles/20040128/Feature1.asp
This web page provides a good explanation of animal cloning.

On Human Cloning: Three Views
www.pbs.org/wgbh/nova/baby/cloning.html
This PBS website presents three different cloning arguments from three scientists, all of whom are experts on the subject.

TOPICS TO LEARN MORE ABOUT

- **Genetically modified (GM) foods**
  In this book you've learned about some of the issues and controversies surrounding cloned foods. Research other forms of genetic modification in the food industry. What are the benefits according to supporters? What kinds of drawbacks do the critics see? Compare and contrast genetically modified food with cloned food.
- **Saving endangered animals**
  As you have seen, there have been attempts to use cloning to save endangered animal species. But some critics argue that this is not the best option. Do further research on this issue to find out what the experts think. What arguments are made in favour of cloning endangered animals? What arguments are made in opposition?

INDEX